Which Way Forward

No Nonsense Life Observations From A Father To His Children

Alan M. Simpson

Copyright Information

How the book started

As a parent, Alan M. Simpson found his children had all too quickly become young adults, and he had a limited amount of time to impart certain life wisdom to his children. He realized that it would never be possible for him to have every meaningful conversation he wanted to have with them. He created this book to speak not only to his children but also the children of others, their parents, and anyone who needs life advice and wisdom.

This book gives guidance in the formation and completion of life goals. The author wanted to ensure that his children had a foundation to build on setting and achieve their goals. He points out that the journey through life is not traveled alone and that taking care of others is critical to individual success. He also offers sage advice regarding motivation, inspiration, and dedication.

Topic oriented and easy to read, keep this book of no-nonsense life observations from a father within easy reach.

Dedicated to Duncan, Collin, and Morgan

Contents

Love

Love is an action word meaning doing for others.

Loving others means do the right thing when the opportunity presents itself. Smile, be a pleasant person to be around, offer assistance where it is needed, be respectful.

Childhood is such a critical time for developing the ability to learn love and to show love through action. As parents do, so does the child.

Relationships

Becoming the best of friends is the key to having a long and fruitful life together.

Do not fuss and fight with one another, respect each other, and trust each other.

True love is an action and not funny feelings of puppy love. The puppy love needs to give way to love through your actions as in respect, trust, listening, and doing the simple things.

So many relationships fail because as puppy love starts to fade, the couple cannot transition into showing love by selfless action.

Family

Your siblings are all going to have different life experiences from you, respect one another.

Listen to your siblings, and not at your sibling's, conversations are not, know it best contests.

Willingly come to your sibling's aid when they need help.

Family members often feel free to treat other family members rudely when they would not treat a non family member in such a manner. In many cases, the rude behavior recipients usually siblings or parents are under a lot of stress as they wish to keep the peace between family members. Be aware of how you are treating family members.

Parents

It is not possible to know how much a parent loves you until you become a parent.

The number one thing to keep in mind about your parents is that they are human beings with all the feelings and emotions you have. When you treat them with anger and indifference, it hurts them.

Your parents were raised during a different time in society from you. Since the beginning of the twentieth century, the twenty to thirty-year difference in age between teenage years for parents and children represents ever-increasing societal change. The time in which your parents grew up is not better or worse, just different.

Look back two years and recognize how much knowledge you have gained in those years. Take that knowledge times ten, and you will see just how far ahead of you in learned knowledge your parents are. Respect that knowledge.

Remember that parenting is a learn on the job process. Parents cannot possibly anticipate every situation that will arise during the growing up years. Many times parents are playing catch up to what is happening in their children's lives.

The need for parents never ends.

Raising Children

Be involved with your children. It is guaranteed if you are not someone else is, the world is competing with you for your children.

It doesn't matter what else is going on; you always have time to be a parent. The most important job you will ever have once you have children. If your children begin to feel that they are secondary to your career, they will behave that way.

If you do not have children being a good role model for others children is the most important job you will ever have.

Listen to your children when they want to talk; it is critical to understanding who they are.

Your children cannot make the same decisions as yourself. They lack the benefit of your years of hindsight. The best you can do is share your years of learning and explain the reason why you think a decision should be made a certain way.

When your children are young, get down on their level when you talk to them.

As your children reach into their teenage years your role changes to being a life coach. You are calling plays from the sideline, while they are playing the game of life.

Hug your children, they need it.

Be supportive of your children, not critical of them.

Being a parent never ends no matter how old your children get.

Life Goals

It has been my observation that the path to achieving goals happens in a much more timely manner when you elevate others to success along with yourself. When you advance others, they will be more loyal and more likely to go above and beyond in assisting you.

One person's goal is another person's waste of time. Be self-aware that your goals may seem a waste of time to others before you criticize another's ambitions.

It may seem as though many people do not have goals. You may be surprised that their singular goal is to have a well-lived life. You may also be surprised at how happy these people are.

It is important to thank and reward the people who help you achieve your goals. Many people who have completed their goals are not well respected due to their misusing others while accomplishing their goals.

End of Life

If you have never had an end-of-life conversation with a parent, you have not experienced one of the most profound bonds between parent and child.

When a parent wants to discuss their feelings about the approaching end of life, sit and listen. They need the conversation to help them put it into perspective. You will be the wiser for it.

Suddenly losing a family member or a friend can leave a person searching for a reason why. Sometimes you have to accept the fact that there is no understandable reason why.

After losing a friend or family member, people are so tied up in the busy of laying them to rest that remembering who said what and who was visiting is often lost. Once being busy is over, the person is left dealing with their feelings and memories while life returns to normal for everyone else. The time to send a card or visit is when they are feeling alone and left behind.

Conversation

Mature conversation is a great stress reliever.

Most people want to get things off of their chest, not have you solve their problems. Listen with understanding. Soon enough it will be your turn to blow off steam and move on.

Being humble in conversation allows us to learn from others.

Spend more time asking questions and listening than talking, learning something new from everyone you meet.

The best way to learn the art of conversation is to sit down and talk to an elderly man or woman who is well past having anything to prove in life.

Listen with understanding. You must understand the information and the context in which it was given before you respond. Take just a bit of time to process. Haste causes misunderstandings, thoughtfulness results in clarity.

Maturity

Learning the things, you can change and the things you cannot change is an important step in developing maturity.

Maturity is not an act; it is a way of living. The office clown can be the most mature person in the room.

We all know people who behave as if maturity is a specific type of behavior. In the end, behavior as maturity exposes that person's lack of maturity gained through experience. Maturity comes with experience, be yourself.

Maturity does not mean life is not fun. It is the ability to know when work ends, and play starts.

Your Legacy

You do not get to say what your legacy is going to be, but you can have an effect on your legacy by the life you lead.

All too often, as life is nearing its end, people spend time and money trying to ensure their legacy. It is too late as the body of their life's work is behind them.

Money

Money and things are nice to have but a weak foundation on which to build a life. Take note of the people around you for whom the accumulation of money and things is a priority. Notice how once a monetary goal is met, it is never enough. Life for them is a rush from goal to goal, never reaching a point of happiness and satisfaction.

Start a retirement account early, so you at least have a choice of working or retirement in your golden years.

Money is quick to spend but takes time to earn.

Pay fair market value for goods and services. A lifetime of undercutting others is in poor taste at best and harmful to people needing a fair market value for their products and services at worst.

Caring

For most people being a positive influence, every day will have the most significant impact on more people than trying to do big things. Do the small things.

Too busy doing good to be good. In other words, doing good to be seen is less effective and rewarding than being good when no one is watching.

To take care of others, you must first take care of yourself both physically and mentally. Taking care of yourself does not mean be selfish; it means to give your best; you must be at your best.

People will first remember how you made them feel.

Be empathetic, listen to people, not at people.

Honesty

If someone asks how you're doing and you are having a bad day, say you're having a bad day. Why misstate the truth. If people cannot handle honesty, then that is their problem. Life is not perfect, kind of a waste to pretend it is.

Honesty is critical in your relationships with others.

There are times when it is necessary to withhold pieces of information for various reasons, and sometimes silence is golden, but not being deceptive is critical.

Do not pretend to be a person you are not. People will know.

Once you lose the position of being an honest person, it is hard to get back.

It is a mistake to assume you would not be in the other person's position; you have the benefit of their hindsight.

Live Humbly

At times it is best to turn the other cheek, and at times it is best to stand your ground. Learning which action is best can take a lifetime.

Treat others as you want to be treated. We all fail at this from time to time, and when we do, it does not make us bad people. The important thing is to recognize when we fail and to use the failure for improvement.

It can be challenging to balance being humble with bragging during those times where we need to express our accomplishments.

Leave ego at the door. There is no room for personal growth if a person cannot learn from the people around them.

Mistakes

A mistake is only a waste of time if you did not learn from the experience.

We all make mistakes. If you ever wondered where older people get their wisdom, it is from a lifetime of making mistakes and learning from those mistakes.

Many people try to hide their mistakes and therefore never learn from them. They do not realize that their lack of personal growth does show.

It is important that you allow others to make mistakes. They need the opportunity to learn and grow for themselves.

Giving

There is a time when receiving is equal to giving. Many people want to return a favor or give back after you have done something beneficial for them. It is ok to decline their offer politely one maybe two times, but then you must accept their offer. Their return offer means as much to them as your initial act did to you.

We live in a time where "giving" must be termed "giving back". Giving back means you are returning a gift given to you. Giving means you are using your resources to help others. Do not be shamed into calling your gift, giving back. The two actions have two different meanings.

Friends

To be a true friend, you need to be willing to offer your help on the days you would rather be doing something else. The helping role needs to go both ways to be a true friendship.

Sometimes you need to leave behind friends who only take from you, leaving you drained from the constant effort of propping them up.

As an adult, most friendships are made in college or the adult world.

It is rare for pre-college friends to remain in contact. Childhood and teenage ideals between friends have a hard time surviving the transition to adulthood.

I was reading the comments of a Stand By Me movie video clip. The ending of the movie has a significant impact on the adults that watch it. Many are melancholy over the fact that friends have come and gone. Some would have loved to have remained friends, but the friends drifted away. Others are no longer trusting enough to kindle new friendships. The following is a quote from the comments, "Adults don't do friendship well. Do they?".

Learning

Remember it is only a waste of time if you did not learn from the experience.

Never in history has so much knowledge been available to you for decision making.

Teach children how to learn, how to read, and how to problem-solve, and you have set them up for life.

Learning is an additive process. You do not replace what you know with something new; you add to what you know with something new.

It is important to know what you do not know.

We all have our way of learning, pay attention to how you learn best, and apply that when you need to learn new things.

Not a Defect

- A difference in personality is not a personal defect.
- A difference in income level is not a personal defect.
- A difference in education level is not a personal defect.
- A difference in job position is not a personal defect.
- A difference in upbringing is not a personal defect.
- A difference in a person's race is not a personal defect.

These differences are the most extraordinary of things, being human.

Another of the most human of things is to use those and other differences to elevate oneself to a level of self-importance over others. Perhaps, just perhaps the real defect lies in self-importance.

Groups

Being a member of a group or organization has its benefits.

It is essential to maintain independent thinking and avoid joining group think.

Being a participant in group think narrows a person's view of the world. Members of the group begin to feel that their group is special in some way. They begin to interact differently with people outside of the group, usually in a negative manner. Groups exist in many different forms socioeconomic, workplace, religious, charity, etc. and they all can form the belief that they are special to the rest of society and begin to behave that way.

Being a Leader

You may find yourself becoming the unintentional leader.

A leader knows when work is too getting stressful, stops the work orders in pizza, and gives their workers a break.

A leader is a person who lifts the people around themselves; leadership does not require being in charge.

Many times, people who are authentic and caring become unofficial leaders at work or in their peer group.

A leader is not there to tell people what to do. A leader is there to give direction to the people in their department. To provide the tools necessary for the people in their department to accomplish the task at hand.

While the principles of leadership can be taught in a classroom, effective leadership can only be exercised by truly believing in and living those principles.

Think back to a favorite supportive teacher or a favorite supportive boss. You most likely cannot name anything specific that person did to make them a favorite. When done properly results of true servant leadership are essentially hidden. A servant leader is not imposing themselves on others but is teaching others how to grow and develop themselves. This style of leadership does not leave behind a trail of breadcrumbs leading back to the servant leader. Rather than looking for accolades, the servant leader takes satisfaction in observing the growth of the people around them.

Work

Do your best work, not for your employer, not for your customer but for yourself.

Many people look at a job as if they work for the company and the company is in control, but you don't work for the company, you are working for yourself. What you have done is make a contract with the company to trade your skills and your knowledge for their pay and compensation package. That puts you back in control or at least a level playing field and not the company. If you look at it as a two-way contract, then any future company that you may contract with, the control will always belong to you and not the company.

People will value their own work over the work of others.

Defining Success

At the time of this writing, Americans define success by the acquisition of wealth and material goods. Being wealthy is not a defect on its own; it is the life lived on the way to becoming wealthy that is important. Too many Americans tend to pay no attention to what they are doing to others in their quest for "success."

It appears from observation when the goal is wealth as each level of becoming wealthy becomes achieved, it is never enough. Wealth achievers being less satisfied with life than people who put more effort into living a life doing their best and of sharing with others.

I do not know of a single person who is truly a self-made success. Everyone is relying on the knowledge of others directly or indirectly.

History

You are not responsible for the actions of your ancestors. They lived in a time and place different than your own.

History is filtered by time. Every generation between you and the events of history adds its filter to the interpretation of events.

Remember, you are a witness to the history of your time. Your interpretation of what you have witnessed is how you will pass history to future generations. Other people are going to have a different understanding of the same events than you. When you see the differences, then you begin to understand why history is not set in stone.

Politics

Understanding how the government interacts with citizens is concerning to many people, explaining why arguments get so heated.

Family bonds are far more important than arguments over politics.

Politics does not bring families closer together, but arguments over politics can tear families apart.

It is said that discretion is the better part of valor; in the same vein, discretion is the better part of politics. Knowing when and where to discuss politics is critical to happy families, strong friendships, and peaceful work environments.

Recognize that life experience will change your view of politics.

Drinking Alcohol

Our family has had the unfortunate experience of losing a family member, Helen, to a drunk driver. The "killer" of Helen did not set out to kill her that day, but the effects of him drinking too much were that they met in a head-on car crash on a lonely West Texas highway.

I cannot stress enough that the downsides of drinking too much alcohol can be the death of one or more people.

Watch a video of a drunk driver being arrested and ask yourself if that is something you would want to experience.

You have a choice; choose wisely.

In Conclusion

My goal has not been to tell you how to live life. Life is to be lived by the individual, each having their own experiences. My goal is to give a foundation for you to reference and on which to build. In the end, people do not remember how much money you had; they remember how you lived your life and how you made them feel. Your legacy is not built in a day. It is built in a lifetime. Draw from my journey as you create your own unique journey.

Alan M. Simpson